TURN A *recipe* INTO A *formula*
AND CREATE *endless* POSSIBILITIES

THE FORMULA
Cookbook

recipes by
Megan Dow

design by
Coral Barajas

+

+ Protein

+ Something Creamy

+ Flavor Blast

+ mix in

+ Something Sweet

+ Spice It Up

Table of Contents
The Formula Cookbook

Introduction
The Formula Cookbook

Two ambitious moms collaborate to solve one of the biggest problems for families at mealtime. Have you ever said, "I really want to make that recipe, but I don't have all the ingredients," or "I wish I could just make one meal that satisfies everyone"?

Whether you have picky eaters, food allergies, intolerances, celiac disease, diabetes or you just don't have the exact ingredients a recipe calls for, *The Formula Cookbook* will solve any mealtime dilemma!

Meg's Story

My love for cooking started when I was a young child. Making chocolate chip cookies with my mom is one of my favorite memories. She has encouraged me ever since; my family has many great cooks who have taught me to love food and appreciate cooking.

In college, I studied hospitality and tourism management with an emphasis in restaurant and event management and was required to fulfill two internships. The president of the department was generous in allowing me to have one of my mandatory internships at an upscale hotel in San Diego, California. There I worked in different culinary outlets within the hotel, learning everything from catering events for 500 people to making sushi in the outlet restaurant. I knew that I loved cooking and creating new recipes.

After my internship, I became a personal chef and had my own catering company. I absolutely loved being a personal chef. I truly had the best clients and each of them holds a special place in my heart.

After graduating from college, I decided to go to culinary school. So I packed up my bags, put my business on hold, and went to Apicius Culinary School in Florence, Italy. This was one of the best decisions of my life (other than marrying my husband and having my children). I not only loved going to culinary school, but I also loved being in Italy.

When I came back from Italy, I continued with my business. I taught cooking classes at cooking stores and in schools. I then took a job with a company as a restaurant consultant chef where I created new recipes for start-ups as well as established restaurants around the country. I found my passion of developing recipes.

I left the restaurant consulting company to have a family and now have an amazing husband and two beautiful boys who keep me busy creating recipes for them.

Coral's Story

First and foremost, I am a wife and a mom of four amazing children. I also work in the medical field as an Obstetric and Gynecological Sonographer. My passion is helping people during the happiest as well as some of the darkest of times. Having seen so much in the medical field, I am amazed at how precious our bodies and how blessed the gift of life is.

Almost two years ago my third daughter was diagnosed with celiac disease after her second birthday. As hard and confusing as that diagnosis was, I decided that I wanted to master what a celiac life looks like and all that it entails. I created a positive and raw social media account where I was able to post products, encouragement, our journey and the every-day life of a family with celiac disease. I never wanted my little Chanelle to feel that she was anything less because of her diagnosis. Instead, she truly feels the opposite. She has an amazing positive attitude and never complains if she can't have something that someone else is eating. She is such a great example of finding joy in difficult times.

In this journey, I have learned that my youngest daughter and I are both severely allergic to gluten as well. Neither of us have active celiac disease at this time, but we both carry the gene. My other children have different food allergies that makes cooking quite an adventure in my home.

While serving the celiac community, I linked up with Meg, an amazing friend and chef, to offer gluten-free cooking classes. Those classes were such a hit, that we realized the need to work together, and we created a food allergy gaming app. We recognized the need to help not only those with celiac disease, but those with food allergies, intolerances, or any other restricted food diets. We want to help as many people as possible.

2 Mom's

Together we are two moms trying to make a difference in the world. We know how hard it can be to prepare a meal for multiple tastes, diets, and restrictions and we are here to change that. *The Formula Cookbook* revolutionizes how families look at cooking and how they can manage all their meal-time struggles, whether it is for people with food allergies, picky eaters, novice cooks or experienced chefs. Everyone can benefit from this original concept of turning a recipe into a formula to create endless possibilities.

This cookbook is literally for EVERYONE! Our hope is that you use *The Formula Cookbook* to feed your family delicious meals and enjoy the process.

How Formulas Work

The Formula Cookbook

Have you ever found yourself making MORE than one meal at a time? We have several friends who cook a different meal for each person in their family. We just can't sit back without helping. This cookbook is going to change the way YOU cook. *The Formula Cookbook* will also change the way you think about cooking and the way you feed your family and friends. No more making multiple meals for one siting.

Our formulas give multiple options with each recipe to give you a solution to any of your meal time troubles: whether that's dietary restrictions, food allergies or picky eaters. These recipes give you options for everyone. If someone has to eat gluten free, choose the gluten-free options. If someone doesn't like quinoa, choose the rice instead. It's that easy!

By turning a recipe for pancakes into a formula, you can create hundreds of different flavored pancake options and also cater to food allergies or those on restricted diets, using different base, liquid, mix in and flavor-blast options. You can choose different combinations to please your entire family.

Our recipes are designed to make multiple mouth-watering, crowd-pleasing meals. *The Formula Cookbook* is your guide to become creative in the kitchen.
See an example on page 10.

Food Allergies
The Formula Cookbook

•••••••••••••••••••••••••••

Food allergies, celiac disease, or any other dietary restrictions can cause so much stress at meal time. Trust us, we live it. *The Formula Cookbook* has transformed the way we cook and the way we feel about cooking allergen friendly. The symbols below are your guide to pick gluten free and dairy free options.

Allergy Symbols:

GF = gluten free
DF = dairy free

For protein, vegetable, and fruit allergies, simply choose a different choice within the formula. For example, if you are allergic to pineapple use an apple ring instead of a pineapple ring in the pancake recipe for a yummy apple pie pancake option. Or if you can't have chicken, use a beef option in the skewers formula. See how easy it is? We are here to help you find your groove.

Coral manages multiple food allergies within her home which used to be a planning nightmare. Meal times were a hot mess and a huge stress with a child who has celiac disease and other children with egg, dairy, chicken, and nut allergies and intolerances. She would make multiple safe meals for her children, now with *The Formula Cookbook* she makes one meal that satisfies and is safe for everyone. She chooses a recipe she would like to make, then looks at the formula and substitutes anything she needs to fit her family's dietary needs.

For more resources about food allergies, intolerances or celiac disease you can check out our website www.AllergyReality.com. You will find tips, tricks, inspiration, and so much more!

•••••••••••••••••••••••••

Example Formula
The Formula Cookbook

The Sample Recipe

Directions

Here are your step by step directions. You can swap out any of the highlighted items you choose from the formula.

The Formula

This is where you learn how to create different flavor profiles or adjust for dietary restrictions. Pick your desired option within each category. If there is not a number next to the category feel free to choose as many items from the list you desire.

Example Formula
The Formula Cookbook

Pancake Formula

1 BASE	+	1 LIQUID	+	1 FLAVOR BLAST	+	MIX INS	+	TOPPINGS
Pancake Mix:		(DF) Coconut Milk		**Dry Instant Pudding**		**Carrots, Shredded**		Fruit
Regular		(DF) **Almond Milk**		**Mix:**		**Zucchini, Shredded**		**Nuts**
Whole Wheat		(DF) **Cashew Milk**		Vanilla		**Banana**		Shredded Coconut
(GF) Gluten Free		(DF) **Soy Milk**		**Chocolate**		**Apple Sauce**		**Chocolate Chips**
		Milk		**Lemon**		**Seeds**		
						Citrus Zest		

(GF) = Gluten Free   (DF) = Dairy Free

Pick from each category to create your new recipe. If there is not a number in front of the item
you can use as many of the choices as you like.

For example...

1 Base: Gluten Free Pancake Mix
1 Liquid: Almond Milk
1 Flavor Blast: Lemon Pudding Mix
Mix Ins: Poppyseeds, Lemon Zest
Toppings: No Thanks!

We have now created a gluten free lemon poppyseed pancake!

Base: Whole Wheat
Liquid: Almond Milk
Flavor Blast: Vanilla Pudding Mix
Mix Ins: Shredded Carrots
Toppings: Pecans

We have now created a carrot cake pancake!

Kitchen Additions
The Formula Cookbook

• •

Pantry Essentials

Cooking is easy when you have the right tools and ingredients. We recommend building up your kitchen and pantry little by little. Each time you go to the market pick up something new from our pantry essentials list. You will see a huge difference when you have a stocked pantry with key ingredients and the right tools you need.

I also like to keep my freezer stocked with essentials. I usually make a run to my local food warehouse store once a month to buy items in bulk like meat, poultry, fish and cheese. I portion each item into ziplock bags and pop them in the freezer with the date. A pound of meat usually goes pretty far for a family of four. If you have a bigger family you can portion out how much your family eats in one sitting and if you like leftovers, then account for that as well. Using this plan can reduce your grocery budget. You can also stock up when you see an item like ground beef on sale at the supermarket. Most items last up to six months in the freezer, stored air tight.

Tool Essentials

Kitchen tools are essential for cooking. My rule of thumb is to invest in higher quality items such as knives and pans rather than getting the most expensive peeler or grater. Spend more on the items you use everyday. You can check out our recommendations for tools on our YouTube channel, *Allergy Reality*.

Pantry Essentials List

Baking Essentials

Flour
Granulated Sugar
Brown Sugar
Powdered Sugar
Baking Powder
Baking Soda
Instant Dry Pudding Mix
Vanilla Bean Paste or Extract
Chocolate Chips
Pancake Mix
Brownie Mix
Cake Mix
Honey
Maple Syrup

Canned Foods

Tomatoes
Black Beans
Pinto Beans
Refried Beans
Chicken Stock
Vegetable Stock
Pureed Pumpkin
Olives
Corn
Pineapple
Peaches

Dried Goods

Panko Bread Crumbs
Dried Fruits
Nuts
Shredded Coconut

Grains and Pasta

White Rice
Brown Rice
Quinoa
Pasta
Gluten Free Pasta
Rolled Oats
Oatmeal

Oils and Vinegars

Olive Oil
Vegetable or Canola Oil
Coconut Oil
Red Wine Vinegar
White Wine Vinegar
Balsamic Vinegar

Sauces and Jarred Foods

Ketchup
Yellow Mustard
Dijon Mustard
Worchestershire Sauce
Hoisin Sauce
Teriyaki Sauce
Buffalo Hot Sauce
Jarred Salsa
Jarred Alfredo Sauce
Jarred Tomato Sauce
Jam
Jelly
Peanut Butter

Herbs and Spices

Kosher Salt
Black Pepper
Garlic Salt
Cumin
Chili Powder
Taco Seasoning
Onion Powder
Cinnamon
Italian Seasoning

arge non-stick sauté pan
mall non-stick sauté pan
1 grill pan
1 saucepan with lid
1 muffin pan
2 cake pans, 8 inch
glass baking dish 9x12
tic cutting boards with grips
1 large mixing bowl
1 small mixing bowl

Tool Additions
The Formula Cookbook

· ·

1 chef's knife
1 serrated knife
1 pairing knife
zester
grater
spatulas
serving spoons
ladle
potato smasher
tongs
whisk
peeler
can opener
measuring cups
measuring spoons
pot holders
ice cream scoop
kitchen towels

+ Something
Creamy

+ Flavor
Blast

+ Protein

+ Spice
It Up

+ mix
in

+ Something
Sweet

Breakfast
Formulas

. . . .

MUFFINS

BREAKFAST BURRITOS

OATMEAL

MINI FRITTATA

PANCAKES

SMOOTHIE BOWLS

PARFAIT

. . . .

 Formula

1 BASE   +   1 LIQUID   +   1 FLAVOR BLAST   +   MIX INS

(GF) Flour

All Purpose
  Flour
Whole Wheat
  Flour
Muffin Mix

Milk
Buttermilk
(DF) Almond Milk
(DF) Coconut Milk

Dry Instant Pudding
  Mix:
  Vanilla
  Banana
  Lemon
  Chocolate

Nuts
Shredded Coconut
Fruit
Chocolate Chips
Citrus Zest

(GF) = Gluten Free   (DF) = Dairy Free

(GF) Blueberry Orange Muffins

Makes 1 Dozen

INGREDIENTS

Cooking Spray
1/2 Cup Unsalted Butter, Softened
1 Cup Granulated Sugar
1/4 Cup Brown Sugar
2 Eggs
1/2 Cup Dry Instant Vanilla Pudding Mix
1/2 Cup Buttermilk
1 1/2 Cups (GF) Flour
2 Teaspoons Baking Powder
1/2 Teaspoon Kosher Salt
1 Teaspoon Vanilla Extract or Vanilla
   Bean Paste
1/2 Teaspoon Orange Zest
1 Tablespoon Orange Juice
1 1/2 Cup Frozen Blueberries

GLAZE INGREDIENTS

3/4 Cup Powdered Sugar
2 Tablespoons +1 Teaspoon Orange Juice

GLAZE DIRECTIONS

1 Combine powdered sugar and orange juice in a small mixing bowl.

2 Drizzle glaze over cooled muffins with a fork or a spoon.

DIRECTIONS

1 Preheat oven to 425° F. Spray muffin tin with cooking spray or line with paper baking cups.

2 In a large mixing bowl cream the butter and the sugars together until light and fluffy. Add one egg at a time, making sure the egg is completely mixed into the batter.

3 In a medium size bowl mix together flour, baking powder and salt.

4 Add the vanilla pudding mix and half of the flour mixture and stir until combined. Add the buttermilk and stir to combine. Add the remaining amount of flour along with vanilla extract, orange zest and juice and stir until combined.

5 Fold in the blueberries. Scoop 1/4 cup of the batter into the muffin tins. Place in the oven and immediately reduce the heat to 375°F. Bake for 20-25 minutes. Remove from oven and let cool in the pan. When muffins have cooled, follow the glaze directions.

Bacon Cheddar Burritos

Makes 6 Egg Burritos

INGREDIENTS

6 Flour Tortillas
2 Tablespoons Olive Oil
2 Cups Frozen Hash Browns
Cooking Spray
12 Eggs
12 Slices Black Forest Bacon, Cooked, Diced
2 Cup Cheddar Cheese, Shredded
Salt and Pepper to Taste
1 Tablespoon Chives, Finely Chopped

DIRECTIONS

1 Preheat oven to 375°F. Cook the tortillas over an open flame to slightly grill and to become pliable (about 30 seconds).

2 In a large non-stick sauté pan on medium heat, heat 2 tablespoons olive oil for 1 minute or until hot. Add hash browns and cook on high for 5 minutes (do not stir). Once hash browns have browned on one side, flip and cook on the other side for 5 minutes. Remove from pan and set aside.

3 Crack the eggs in a mixing bowl and wisk with a fork.

4 Add more oil to the pan if needed or spray with cooking spray. Pour egg mixture into the pan and gently pull eggs across the pan until small curds appear. Continue to cook pulling, lifting and folding eggs until no visible liquid egg remains.

5 Add the bacon, hash browns and cheddar cheese into the pan, combine and stir to incorporate. Add salt and pepper to taste and the chives and remove from heat.

6 Place the cooked tortilla in the middle of a 12" piece of foil or parchment paper. Place 1/2 cup of the egg mixture in the center of the tortilla, fold over sides and roll to form a burrito. Continue until all of the egg mixture is gone and place the burritos in a large ziplock bag. Place in the freezer for up to 3 months or serve immediately.

• •

I like to pick one day of the month where I prepare all of my freezer meals. This makes my life easier for the whole month! One of my favorites are these Freezer breakfast burritos. When ready to serve from the freezer, remove from foil and microwave on high for 1 1/2 - 2 minutes.

Breakfast Burrito Formula

1 WRAP IT UP	+	1 BASE	+	1 STARCH	+	MIX INS
GF Flour Tortilla		Whole Eggs		Potato		Meat Choice
Flour Tortilla		Egg Whites		Hash Browns		Cheese Choice
Corn Tortilla		Liquid Eggs		Tater Tots		DF Cheese
Lavash				Rice		Vegetable Choice
				Mexican Rice		Herb Choice
				Fried Rice		Avocado
						Salsa

GF = Gluten Free   DF = Dairy Free

Oatmeal is one of the healthiest breakfasts you can eat! It's packed with fiber and it keeps you full for a long time. If you are in a pinch you can make this recipe in a glass jar the night before, refrigerate it, and take it on the go in the morning.

Peaches and Cream Oatmeal

Makes 1 Serving

INGREDIENTS

1/2 Cup Quick Cooking Oats
1/2 Cup Vanilla Almond Milk
1/2 Cup Vanilla Yogurt
1/2 Cup Fresh Peaches, Cut Into Cubes
Cinnamon (to taste)

FAN FAVORITE FORMULA

Base: (GF) Oats
Liquid: Coconut Milk
Creamy: Whipped Cream
Mix Ins: Chocolate Chips & Shredded Coconut
Flavor Blast: Vanilla Extract

DIRECTIONS

1. Place the oats in your serving bowl.

2. In a small saucepan on medium heat, bring the almond milk to a simmer (about 1 minute) and remove from heat.

3. Pour the milk over the oats and stir until liquid is absorbed.

4. Top with yogurt, fresh peaches and cinnamon.

Oatmeal Formula

1 BASE	+	1 LIQUID	+	1 CREAMY	+	MIX INS	+	FLAVOR BLAST
Quick Oats		Milk		Yogurt		Fruit		Citrus Zest
(GF) Oats		(DF) Almond Milk		(DF) Yogurt		Chocolate Chips		Spices
Quinoa		(DF) Cashew Milk		Whipping Cream		Shredded Coconut		Extracts
Chia Seeds		(DF) Coconut Milk				Nuts		
Cream of Wheat		(DF) Soy Milk				Flax Seed		
Cooked Rice		Water				Chia Seeds		
						Honey		

(GF) = Gluten Free   (DF) = Dairy Free

(GF) Mini Frittata *Formula*

1 BASE	+	MIX INS	+	FLAVOR BLAST
Whole Eggs		Cheese Choice		Pesto
Egg Whites		(DF) Cheese		Salsa
Liquid Eggs		Vegetable Choice		Seasonings
		Meat Choice		Herb Choice

(GF) = Gluten Free   (DF) = Dairy Free

Sausage and Cheese Mini Frittatas

Makes 1 Dozen

INGREDIENTS

Cooking Spray
12 Eggs
1 Cup Cheddar Cheese, Shredded
6 Sausage Links, Roughly Chopped
Kosher Salt and Pepper To Taste

FAN FAVORITE FORMULA

Base: Egg Whites
Mix Ins: Spinach, Sundried Tomato & Feta
Flavor Blast: Pesto

DIRECTIONS

1 Preheat the oven to 350°F. Spray the muffin tin pan with non-stick cooking spray.

2 Crack the eggs into a medium mixing bowl and whisk with a fork.

3 Evenly pour the egg mixture into the muffin tins.

4 Top each muffin tin with cheese and sausage.

5 Bake for 15 minutes.

6 Remove from oven and season with salt and pepper.

I love eggs, but I don't always feel like cooking eggs in the morning. These frittatas are great because you can keep them in the fridge and then pop them in the microwave for 20-30 seconds for a quick and healthy breakfast. You can also place them in between some English muffins with a slice of cheese and freeze them for an easy breakfast sandwich. Just pop them straight from the freezer to the microwave and you have another fast healthy breakfast option.

⑤ Piña Colada Pancakes

Makes 4 Servings

INGREDIENTS

1 1/2 Cup ⑤ Pancake Mix
1/2 Cup Dry Instant Vanilla Pudding Mix
2 Eggs
1/4 Cup Vegetable Oil
2 Cups ⑤ Coconut Milk
Cooking Spray
4 Rings Fresh Pineapple, Sliced 1/8 Inch

TOPPINGS

1/2 Cup Fresh Pineapple, Cubed 1/4"
Maraschino Cherries
2 Tablespoons Sweetened, Shredded
    Coconut, Toasted

COCONUT SYRUP INGREDIENTS

1 (14) Ounce Can Sweetened
    Condensed Milk
1/2 Teaspoon Coconut Extract
1/2 Teaspoon Butter Extract

SYRUP DIRECTIONS

1 Mix together all the ingredients in a microwave safe bowl.

2 Microwave for 30 seconds to warm.

DIRECTIONS

1 Preheat a nonstick griddle or nonstick sauté pan on medium heat.

2 Place pancake mix and dry pudding mix in a medium mixing bowl. Add eggs, vegetable oil and coconut milk and mix until combined (do not over mix).

3 Spray the griddle or nonstick pan with cooking spray. Place the rings of pineapple in the pan (make sure you have space between your pineapple rings). Add 1/4 cup of the pancake batter over each pineapple ring covering the pineapple completely.

4 Follow syrup directions listed above.

5 Cook for 5-7 minutes. Flip the pancake with a spatula and cook on the other side for 3 minutes. Remove from heat and top with syrup, fresh pineapple, shredded coconut and a maraschino cherry.

Pancake *Formula*

I BASE	+	I LIQUID	+	I FLAVOR BLAST	+	MIX INS	+	TOPPINGS

Pancake Mix:
  Regular
  Whole Wheat
  (GF) Gluten Free
		(DF) Coconut Milk
		(DF) Almond Milk
		(DF) Cashew Milk
		(DF) Soy Milk
		Milk
				Dry Instant
				Pudding Mix:
				  Vanilla
				  Chocolate
				  Lemon
						Carrots, Shredded
						Zucchini, Shredded
						Banana
						Apple Sauce
						Seeds
						Citrus Zest
								Fruit
								Nuts
								Shredded
								  Coconut
								Chocolate
								  Chips

(GF) = Gluten Free   (DF) = Dairy Free

(GF) Mango Smoothie Bowl

Makes 1 Bowl

I love smoothie bowls! This is a great breakfast, lunch or snack.

INGREDIENTS

1 Frozen Banana
1/2 Cup Frozen Mango
1/2 Cup Frozen Pineapple
2/3 Cup Orange Juice
1/4 Cup Frozen Strawberries
1/4 Cup Vanilla Yogurt
1 Tablespoon Chia Seeds

TOPPINGS

Chia Seeds
Kiwi
Mango
Shredded Coconut
Strawberries

DIRECTIONS

1 Place all the ingredients in a blender and blend on high for 45 seconds. Make sure it is completely smooth.

2 Place smoothie in a serving bowl and top with toppings.

Smoothie Bowl *Formula*

1 BASE	+	FROZEN FRUIT	+	1 LIQUID	+	VITAMIN BOOST	+	TOPPINGS
Greek Yogurt		Bananas		Orange Juice		Greens		Fresh Fruit
Flavored		Pineapple		Cranberry Juice		Powdered		Nuts
Yogurt		Mango		Pineapple Juice		Collagen		Shredded
(DF) Yogurt		Blueberries		Apple Juice		Protein Powder		Coconut
		Raspberries		(DF) Coconut Milk		Spirulina		Chocolate Chips
		Strawberries		(DF) Almond Milk				Honey
		Cherries						Chia Seeds
								Flaxseed

(GF) = Gluten Free   (DF) = Dairy Free

29

ⓖⒻ Peanut Butter Chocolate Parfait

Makes 1 Serving

INGREDIENTS

1 **Cup** Greek Yogurt
1/4 **Teaspoon** Vanilla Bean Paste or Vanilla Extract
2 **Tablespoons** Peanut Butter
1 **Tablespoon** Honey
1 Banana, **Sliced**
2 **Tablespoons** Chocolate Chips

DIRECTIONS

1 In a small bowl combine the yogurt with vanilla, peanut butter and honey.

2 Place half of the yogurt in a glass cup or bowl.

3 Top the yogurt with half of the sliced banana.

4 Top with 1 tablespoon chocolate chips.

5 Repeat and serve.

𝒫arfait *Formula*

1 BASE	+	MIX INS	+	TOPPINGS
Flavored Yogurt		Peanut Butter		Fruit
ⒹⒻ Yogurt		Jelly or Jam		Chocolate Chips
Greek Yogurt		Honey		Graham Crackers
Prepared Pudding		Fruit		Shredded Coconut
Cool Whip		Lemon Curd		Cake, Crumbled
Coco Whip		Citrus Zest		Cookies, Crumbled
Ice Cream				

ⒼⒻ = Gluten Free   ⒹⒻ = Dairy Free

+ Something
Creamy

+ Protein

+ Flavor
Blast

+ Spice
It Up

+ mix
in

+ Something
Sweet

Lunch
Formulas

· ·

WRAP IT UP

QUESADILLA

CHICKEN FINGERS

SALAD

PANINI

BOWL

FLATBREAD

· ·

Wrap it Up *Formula*

I WRAP IT UP +	I PROTIEN +	I MAKE IT SAUCY +	MIX INS
Flour Tortilla	Rotisserie Chicken	BBQ Sauce	Vegetable
GF Tortilla	Lunch Meat	Pesto	Choice
Lavash	Ground Turkey	Hummus	Cheese Choice
Lettuce	Ground Beef	Mayonnaise	*DF* Cheese
	Steak	Mustard	Lettuce Choice
	Fish	Dressing Choice	Herb Choice

GF = Gluten Free   *DF* = Dairy Free

GF Turkey Pesto Wrap

Makes 1 Wrap

INGREDIENTS

1 GF Tortilla Wrap
1 Tablespoon Pesto
2 Slices Smoked Turkey
1 Slice Provolone Cheese
1 Tablespoon Red Onion, Shaved
2 Tablespoons Red Bell Pepper, Sliced
1/2 Cup Arugula

DIRECTIONS

1. Place the wrap on a clean work surface. Spread pesto evenly in the middle of the wrap.

2. Top with turkey, cheese, red onion, bell pepper and arugula. Roll the tortilla to create a wrap and cut in half.

FAN FAVORITE FORMULA

Base: Lettuce
Make it Saucy: Hummus & Italian Dressing
Protein: Rotisserie Chicken
Toppings: Cucumber, Tomato, Red Onion, Olives & Feta Cheese

Wraps are a go-to lunch in our house. You can use lettuce, tortillas or lavash as great wrap options! This is also a great place to use leftovers from the night before.

35

BBQ Chicken Quesadilla

Makes 2 Servings

INGREDIENTS

2 Flour Tortillas
1/4 Cup BBQ Sauce
1/2 Cup Rotisserie Chicken, Shredded
1/4 Cup Mixed Italian Cheese Blend, Shredded
1 Tablespoon Red Onion, Sliced Thin
1 Teaspoon Cilantro Leaves, Torn

FAN FAVORITE FORMULA

Base: Pita Bread
Something Melty: Blue Cheese & Jack Cheese
Protein: Grilled Steak
Mix In: Arugula

DIRECTIONS

1 Preheat a grill pan or large skillet over medium heat.

2 Place one of the tortillas on a clean work surface.

3 Evenly spread the BBQ sauce on the tortilla and top with chicken, cheese, red onion and cilantro.

4 Top with the other tortilla and carefully place on your grill pan or skillet. Cook for 3-5 minutes per side or until slightly golden and cheese has melted.

5 Transfer to a clean surface and cut into 6 slices.

Quesadilla _Formula_

1 BASE	+	CHEESE	+	1 PROTEIN	+	FLAVOR BLAST	+	MIX IN
Flour Tortilla		Cheese Choice		Grilled Steak		Pesto		Vegetable
(GF) Flour Tortilla		(DF) Cheese		Rotisserie		Buffalo Hot Sauce		Choice
Corn Tortilla				Chicken		Salsa		Fruit Choice
Lavash				Lunch Meat		BBQ Sauce		Lettuce
Pita Bread				Ground Turkey				Herb Choice

(GF) = Gluten Free   (DF) = Dairy Free

Panko Chicken Fingers

Makes 4 Servings

INGREDIENTS

1 Pound Chicken Tenders
2 Tablespoons Pickle Juice
1/2 Teaspoon Kosher Salt
2 Cups Panko Bread Crumbs
1/3 Cup Oil (Peanut, Avocado,
     Vegetable or Coconut)

SPECIAL SAUCE INGREDIENTS

1/2 Cup Mayonnaise
1 Tablespoon BBQ Sauce
1 Teaspoon Yellow Mustard
1 Teaspoon Honey

DIRECTIONS

1. In a small mixing bowl combine all the sauce ingredients until well combined.

DIRECTIONS

1. Marinate chicken tenders in the pickle juice for 2 hours (or up to 24 hours).

2. Preheat a medium size sauté pan or cast iron skillet on medium heat.

3. Place the panko bread crumbs on a plate. Remove the chicken tenders and dredge them in the panko to coat on both sides. Press down to coat.

4. Add the oil to the pan and carefully place the chicken tenders into the hot oil. Cook for 5 minutes on both sides or until cooked through. The crust should be golden brown. Remove from the pan and place on paper towels to drain excess grease. Sprinkle with kosher salt. Serve with special sauce.

Chicken Fingers Formula

1 BASE	+	1 MARINATE IT	+	1 COAT IT	+	DIP IT
Chicken Tenders		Pickle Juice Buttermilk Milk (DF) Milk		(GF) Panko Bread Crumbs Panko Bread Crumbs Italian Bread Crumbs Crunchy Chips Chopped Nuts		Special Sauce Honey Mustard Ketchup BBQ Sauce Sweet Chili Sauce Buffalo Hot Sauce Ranch

(GF) = Gluten Free   (DF) = Dairy Free

Salad
Formula

1 BASE	+	1 PROTEIN	+	MIX INS	+	FLAVOR BLAST
Lettuce Choice		Ground Turkey		Vegetable Choice		Dressing Choice
Grain Choice		Taco Meat		Cheese Choice		Salsa
Pasta Choice		Rotisserie Chicken		(DF) Cheese		Herb Choice
		Steak		Fruit Choice		Shredded Coconut
		Lunch Meat		Nut Choice		
		Beans				

(GF) = Gluten Free   (DF) = Dairy Free

Tropical Chicken Salad

Makes 1-2 Serving

INGREDIENTS

1 Head Butter lettuce, Torn
1/2 Cup Rotisserie Chicken, Sliced or
    Shredded
1/4 Cup Red Bell Pepper, Sliced 1/8 "
1/4 Cup Cucumber, Diced 1/4"
1/4 Cup Mango, Sliced 1/4 " Sticks
1 Tablespoon Mint, Roughly Chopped
2 Tablespoons Whole Cashews
1 Tablespoon Coconut, Shredded,
    Toasted

DRESSING INGREDIENTS

Juice 1 Lime
2 Tablespoons Coconut Milk
1/4 Teaspoon Kosher Salt

DRESSING DIRECTIONS

1 In a small mixing bowl combine lime juice, coconut milk & salt.

2 Serve over Salad.

DIRECTIONS

1 Place clean dried lettuce leaves on a serving plate.

2 Top with chicken, bell pepper, cucumber, mango, mint, cashews and coconut.

3 Follow dressing directions and dress salad with desired amount of dressing. (If using the jar or bag method, see below, place dressing in a separate container until you are ready to eat.)

I love salads! You can make any salad in a jar or in a ziplock bag and take them wherever you go. Make sure you put the dressing in a separate container to keep your salad crisp. Just pour your dressing over the greens and toss it up in the jar or baggie.

Panini Formula

1 BASE + **1 SPREAD** + **1 PROTEIN** + **CHEESE** + **FLAVOR BLAST**

1 BASE	1 SPREAD	1 PROTEIN	CHEESE	FLAVOR BLAST
(GF) Bread	Jam Choice	Lunch Meat	Cheese Choice	Herb Choice
Crusty Rolls	Mustard	Rotisserie Chicken	(DF) Cheese	Fruit
Sliced Bread	Mayonnaise	Bacon		Vegetable Choice
	Chutney	Prosciutto		Buffalo Hot Sauce
	Cream Cheese			Balsamic Glaze
	Pesto			Pickled Jalapeños

(GF) = Gluten Free (DF) = Dairy Free

Rosemary Chicken Panini

Makes 1 Serving

INGREDIENTS

1 Crusty Ciabatta Roll or Other Crusty
    Bread, Cut In Half
1 Tablespoon Fig Jam
2 Slices Provolone Cheese
1/2 Cup Rotisserie Chicken, Shredded
1/4 Teaspoon Fresh Rosemary,
    (removed from stem and finely chopped)
1 Tablespoon Unsalted Butter, Softened

FAN FAVORITE FORMULA

Base: Crusty Roll
Spread: Cream Cheese
Protein: Bacon
Cheese: Cheddar Cheese
Flavor Blast: Pickled Jalepeños

DIRECTIONS

1 Preheat a panini press or a griddle on medium heat.

2 On a clean work surface lay out the bread, cut side up. Spread the fig jam on both sides of the bread.

3 On each side top with a slice of cheese.

4 Place chicken evenly on one side of the bread and sprinkle with rosemary.

5 Place the two pieces together to form a sandwich. Spread with butter on the outside of the bread.

6 Set on the panini press or on a griddle and cook for 3-5 minutes per side or until golden brown. If using a griddle place a plate on top of the panini to weigh it down.

(GF) Quinoa Bowls

Makes 2 Servings

INGREDIENTS

1/4 Cup Rotisserie Chicken, Shredded
3 Tablespoons Salsa Verde
1 Cup Cooked Quinoa

TOPPINGS

2 Tablespoons Guacamole, Pre-made
2 Tablespoons Cheddar Cheese, Shredded
2 Tablespoons Corn Relish (see page 79)
1/4 Cup Romaine, Chopped
1/4 Cup Peppers, Cut in 1/8" Slices, Grilled
1/4 Cup Red Onion, Cut in 1/8" Slices, Grilled
Corn Chips

SALSA RANCH DRESSING INGREDIENTS

1/4 Cup Ranch Dressing
1/4 Cup Red Salsa

SALSA RANCH DRESSING DIRECTIONS

1. In a small mixing bowl, mix together until combined.

DIRECTIONS

1. In a small mixing bowl mix together rotisserie chicken and salsa verde until combined. Heat in the microwave for 1 minute or until hot.

2. Place the quinoa in a serving bowl.

3. Top quinoa with chicken mixture and then top with guacamole, cheese, corn relish, romaine, peppers, onions and corn chips.

4. Follow salsa ranch directions and serve on top of quinoa bowl.

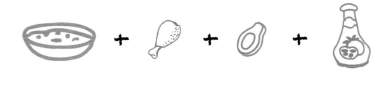

Bowl *Formula*

1 BASE	+	1 PROTEIN	+	TOPPINGS	+	FLAVOR BLAST
Rice		Rotisserie Chicken		Cheese Choice		Dressing Choice
Brown Rice		Fish		(DF) Cheese		Teriyaki Sauce
Quinoa		Beef		Vegetable Choice		Pesto
Pasta		Pork		Chips		Salsa Choice
(GF) Pasta		Ground Turkey		Dried Fruit		Buffalo Hot Sauce
Lettuce				Guacamole		

(GF) = Gluten Free   (DF) = Dairy Free

Flatbread Formula

1 BASE +

Flatbread
(GF) Bread
Pizza Dough
Pita Bread
English Muffins
French Bread

1 MAKE IT SAUCY +

Jam Choice
Pesto
BBQ Sauce
Tomato Sauce
Buffalo Hot Sauce
Peanut Saute Sauce
Hoisin Sauce

TOPPINGS

Cheese Choice
(DF) Cheese
Meat Choice
Vegetable Choice
Fruit Choice
Herb Choice
Citrus Zest
Seasoning Choice
Lettuce

(GF) = Gluten Free   (DF) = Dairy Free

Avocado Lemon Flatbread

Makes 1 Flatbread

INGREDIENTS

1 Flatbread
2 Tablespoons Tomato Sauce
2 Tablespoons Italian Mixed Cheese Blend
1/4 Avocado, Sliced Thin
1 Lemon, Zested
Kosher Salt **(or flaked sea salt) and** Black Pepper
　　To Taste

DIRECTIONS

1　Preheat the oven to 450°F.

2　Place the flatbread on a foil lined baking sheet.

3　Spread the tomato sauce evenly on the flatbread leaving a 1/2 inch edge.

4　Top with cheese and place in the oven for 7-10 minutes or until cheese is melted and slightly golden.

5　Remove the flatbread from the oven and top with sliced avocado, lemon zest, salt and pepper.

I know this sounds like a weird combination but you have to try it! The avocado adds a creaminess and the lemon zest brightens everything up!

+ Something
Creamy

+ Protein

+ Flavor
Blast

+ Spice
It Up

+ mix
in

+ Something
Sweet

Dinner

Formulas

- - - - - - - - - - - - - - - - -

TACOS

CROCKPOT CHICKEN

PASTA

PORK TENDERLOIN

STUFFED POTATOES

SKEWERS

SPAGHETTI SQUASH

HAYSTACKS

TAQUITOS

MEATBALLS

- - - - - - - - - - - - - - - - - -

$\mathcal{Taco}$ Formula

1 BASE	+	1 MAKE IT SAUCY	+	1 PROTEIN	+	TOPPINGS
Corn Tortilla		Salsa Choice		Ground Turkey		Cheese Choice
Flour Tortilla		Teriyaki Sauce		Ground Beef		ⒹⒻ Cheese
ⒼⒻ Flour Tortilla		Buffalo Hot Sauce		Rotisserie Chicken		Vegetable Choice
Lettuce Wrap		Hoisin Sauce		Carne Asada		Herb Choice
				Beans		Hot Sauce
				Steak		Sour Cream
						Rice

ⒼⒻ = Gluten Free   ⒹⒻ = Dairy Free

Salsa Verde Tacos

Makes 6 Tacos

INGREDIENTS

2 **Cups** Rotisserie Chicken, **Shredded**
1 **Cup** Salsa Verde
6 **Corn or** Flour Tortillas

TOPPINGS

Cheddar Cheese, **Shredded**
Pico De Gallo
Cilantro Leaves

FAN FAVORITE FORMULA

Base: Lettuce Wrap
Something Saucy: Red Salsa
Protein: Ground Turkey
Toppings: Cheese, Tomatoes, Olives &
Cilantro

DIRECTIONS

1. Preheat oven to 400°F (If your chicken is still warm skip heating the chicken in the oven).

2. Place the chicken in an oven-proof baking dish.

3. Top the chicken with salsa verde and bake for 5-7 minutes or just until chicken is warmed through.

4. Serve the chicken on the tortillas. Top with desired amount of cheddar cheese, pico de gallo & cliantro leaves.

This is one of my all time favorite dinners and it literally takes 2 minutes to make if your rotisserie chicken is hot. Check out this recipe on Allergy Reality's YouTube Channel for more great tips, titled 'Quick and Easy 2 Minute Chicken Dinner'.

Crockpot Orange Chicken

Makes 6 Servings

INGREDIENTS

2 Pounds Chicken Breasts, Boneless, Skinless
3/4 Cup Orange Marmalade
3/4 Cup Hoisin Sauce
2 Tablespoons Sesame Oil
6 Cups Brown Rice, Cooked

TOPPINGS

Cilantro, Torn
Sesame Seeds

DIRECTIONS

1 Place the chicken breast in a crockpot and set on high for 4 hours.

2 When the chicken is done, remove from the crockpot. Shred the chicken with two forks. Remove any liquid from the crockpot and return the chicken to stay warm.

3 Add the orange marmalade, hoisin sauce and sesame oil to the chicken and mix to combine.

4 Cook your rice to the package directions.

5 Serve the chicken on top of the rice and top with cilantro and sesame seeds.

KIDS FAN FAVORITE FORMULA

Base: Pork Roast
Something Sweet: Brown Sugar
Something Savory: Enchilada Sauce
Toppings: Shredded Cheese, Chives, Olives & Sour Cream

Whenever I cook in the crockpot I cook the meat first, remove all the liquid and fat that comes out and then add the sauces or flavorings. It makes for a much more flavorful dish.

Crockpot Chicken *Formula*

1 BASE	**+**	**1 SWEET**	**+**	**1 SAVORY**	**+**	**TOPPINGS**
Chicken Breast		Jam Choice		Hoisin Sauce		Herb Choice
Pork Roast		Marmalade		BBQ Sauce		Seasonings
Chuck Roast		Brown Sugar		Ketchup		Vegetable Choice
				Dressing Choice		
				Enchilada Sauce		

(GF) = Gluten Free   (DF) = Dairy Free

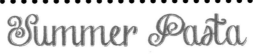

Summer Pasta

Makes 4 Servings

INGREDIENTS

1/4 Cup Frozen Sweet Corn, Thawed
1 Teaspoon Olive Oil
1 Pound Pappardelle Pasta
1/2 Cup Store Bought Pesto
1/2 Cup Heirloom Tomatoes, Diced
1/4 Cup Burrata Cheese, Torn
1/4 Cup Parmesan Cheese, Grated
Black Pepper to Taste

DIRECTIONS

1 Preheat oven to 450°F.

2 Spread the corn on a foil lined baking sheet and drizzle with olive oil. Roast in the oven for 10 minutes.

3 Cook the pasta in boiling, salted water according to package directions. Drain the pasta and return to the pan (Reserve 1/2 cup of the pasta liquid).

4 Add 1/4 cup of the pesto to the cooked pasta. Add the pasta water, roasted corn and tomatoes and stir to combine.

5 Place in the serving dish and top with burrata, parmesan cheese and black pepper.

Pasta Formula

1 BASE	+	1 MAKE IT SAUCY	+	MIX INS
Pasta Choice		Tomato Sauce		Vegetable Choice
(GF) Pasta		Alfredo Sauce		Cheese Choice
Ravioli		Pesto		(DF) Cheese
Tortellini		Butter		Protein Choice
				Fresh Herbs

(GF) = Gluten Free (DF) = Dairy Free

Jam Sauce *Formula*

1 JAM	+	LIQUID	+	SOMETHING TANGY
Blackberry		Juice Choice		Dijon Mustard
Apricot		Stock Choice		Whole Grain Mustard
Mixed Berry		Wine		Cream
Grape				Citrus Zest
Peach				Herb Choice
Fig				

GF = Gluten Free   DF = Dairy Free

(GF) Pork Medallions With Jam Sauce

Makes 4 Servings

INGREDIENTS

1 Pound Pork Medallions, Sliced 1 1/2"
1 Teaspoon Fresh Rosemary, (removed from stem, finely chopped)
1 Teaspoon Kosher Salt
1/2 Teaspoon Black Pepper
1 Tablespoon Avocado Oil or Vegetable Oil
2 Tablespoons Butter

JAM SAUCE INGREDIENTS

1 Cup Fig Jam
1/2 Cup Orange Juice
1/2 Cup Chicken Stock
1 Teaspoon Dijon Mustard
1 Teaspoon Whole Grain Mustard
1/4 Teaspoon Kosher Salt

JAM SAUCE DIRECTIONS

1 In a medium saucepan over medium heat mix the fig jam with orange juice and chicken stock.

2 Add the dijon mustard, whole grain mustard and salt. Cook for 15-20 minutes to reduce slightly and serve.

DIRECTIONS

1 Preheat a cast iron skillet on medium high heat until hot, but not smoking.

2 Season the pork with rosemary, salt and pepper on both sides.

3 Place the oil in the pan and quickly add pork to prevent oil from smoking.

4 Sear the pork for 7 minutes (do not move pork around), flip the pork over and sear for another 7 minutes on the other side.

5 Remove from the heat and equally place butter over the pork medallions. Cover the pan with foil and let sit for 7 minutes in the hot pan. The pork will finish cooking.

6 Follow the sauce directions. Top the pork medallions with sauce.

This recipe can be done with both pork or chicken.
(The formula is for the sauce)

Shepherd Pie Stuffed Potatoes

Makes 6 Servings

INGREDIENTS

6 Russet Potatoes
1 Pound Ground Turkey
1/2 Cup Carrot, Peeled, Diced (about 1 large carrot)
1/2 Stalks Celery, Diced (about 2 stalks)
1/2 Cup White Onion, Diced Small
2 Tablespoons Worcestershire Sauce
1 (15.5) Ounce Can Tomato Sauce
1/2 Teaspoon Kosher Salt
1/8 Teaspoon Black Pepper
1/4 Cup Frozen Peas

> ### FAN FAVORITE FORMULA
>
> **Base:** Sweet Potato
> **Protein:** Shredded Chicken
> **Mix Ins:** Cheese
> **Make it Saucy:** Buffalo Hot Sauce
> **Toppings:** Ranch Dressing

TOPPINGS

Cheddar Cheese, Shredded
Parsley, Chopped

DIRECTIONS

1. Preheat oven to 400°F.

2. Wash and dry the potatoes. Poke holes throughout the potatoes with a fork or knife. Bake the potatoes for 40 minutes.

3. In a large sauté pan or dutch oven cook the ground turkey over medium heat until brown. Remove excess water and fat. Add the carrots, celery and onion. Cook for 5-7 minutes, covered until vegetables are softened.

4. Add worcestershire sauce, tomato sauce, salt and pepper, and cook for 10 minutes to reduce tomato sauce.

5. Add frozen peas and stir to combine.

6. Cut the potatoes in half (lengthwise) and fill each potato with meat mixture. Top with desired amount of cheese. Place under the broiler to melt cheese. Remove and top with parsley.

Stuffed Potatoes
Formula

1 BASE	+	1 PROTEIN	+	MIX INS	+	1 MAKE IT SAUCY	+	TOPPINGS
Russet Potato		Rotisserie Chicken		Vegetable Choice		Alfredo Sauce		Corn Chips
Sweet Potato		Ground Turkey		Seasonings		Buffalo Hot Sauce		Lettuce
Mashed Potatoes		Ground Beef				Salsa		Dressing Choice
		Black Beans				Tomato Sauce		Cheese Choice
		Steak				Pesto		ⒹⒻ Cheese
								Herb Choice

ⒼⒻ = Gluten Free   ⒹⒻ = Dairy Free

Skewers Formula

1 PROTEIN	+	MIX IN	+	SPICE IT UP
Chicken		Vegetable Choice		Marinade Choice
Steak		Fruit Choice		Seasonings
Sausage				Dressing Choice
Lamb				
Shrimp				
Fish				

GF = Gluten Free   DF = Dairy Free

Fajita Skewers

Makes 4 Servings

INGREDIENTS

1 Pound Chicken Breast, Boneless Skinless, Cut in 1" Cubes
1 Green Bell Pepper, Cut in 1" Cubes
1 Red Bell Pepper, Cut in 1" Cubes
1 Yellow Bell Pepper, Cut in 1" Cubes
1 Red Onion, Cut in 1" Cubes
1 Tablespoon Olive Oil
2 Teaspoons Taco Seasoning (of your choice)
1 Teaspoon Kosher Salt
8 Corn Tortillas

TOPPINGS

Cotija Cheese, Crumbled
Cilantro, Torn
Salsa
Salsa Ranch (see page 44)
Lime Wedges

FAN FAVORITE FORMULA

Protein: Sausage, Shrimp
Mix Ins: Corn On The Cobb
Spice It Up: Old Bay Seasoning

DIRECTIONS

1. Soak 8 wooden skewers in water for at least 30 minutes. (You can also use metal skewers)

2. Preheat grill or a grill pan to medium/high heat.

3. Skewer the kebabs on wooden or metal skewers alternating chicken, bell pepper, and onions. Skewer all the chicken, bell peppers and onions.

4. Drizzle the kebabs with olive oil and then season with taco seasoning and salt.

5. Grill for 5-7 minutes per side or until chicken is cooked through.

6. Serve on corn tortillas with the toppings of your choice.

You can literally skewer anything if you think out of the box.
Take a recipe and chances are, you can 'skewer' it.

(GF) Spaghetti Squash

Makes 4 Servings

INGREDIENTS

1 **Pound** Spaghetti Squash
1 **Pound** Ground Turkey
1/2 **Pound** Italian Sausage (removed from casing)
2 **Cups** Jarred Tomato Sauce
1/2 **Teaspoon** Garlic Salt

TOPPINGS

Fresh Basil
Mixed Italian Cheese

FAN FAVORITE FORMULA

Base: Spaghetti Squash
Protein: Shrimp
Make It Saucy: Alfredo Sauce
Mix Ins: Asparagus & Italian Cheese Blend
Toppings: Basil

DIRECTIONS

1. Poke the spaghetti squash with a fork or knife around the whole surface area. Microwave for 7 minutes (If you have a larger spaghetti squash microwave 3 minutes longer).

2. Remove squash from the microwave with a towel to prevent the steam from burning you. Cut in half lengthwise and scoop out the seeds with a fork and discard. Then run the fork along the squash to create strands. Set aside.

3. In a medium sized sauté pan on medium heat brown the ground turkey and sausage and break it up into small pieces with a spatula. Once the meat is cooked through, discard any excess fat. Add the tomato sauce and garlic salt. Cook for an additional 2 minutes and serve over spaghetti squash.

4. Top with cheese and fresh basil.

Spaghetti squash is a great gluten free option for pasta dishes.

Spaghetti Squash *Formula*

I BASE	+	I PROTEIN	+	I MAKE IT SAUCY	+	MIX INS	+	TOPPINGS
Spaghetti Squash		Ground Turkey		Pesto		Cheese Choice		Lettuce
		Ground Beef		Salsa		⒟ⓕ Cheese		Herb
		Shrimp		Tomato Sauce		Vegetable		Choice
		Italian Sausage		Buffalo Hot Sauce		Choice		Corn Chips
		Rotisserie Chicken		Alfredo Sauce				
		Meatballs						

ⓖⓕ = Gluten Free   ⒟ⓕ = Dairy Free

Haystacks Formula

I BASE	+	I PROTEIN	+	I MAKE IT SAUCY	+	TOPPINGS
White Rice		Ground Beef		Cream of Chicken Soup		Cheese Choice
Brown Rice		Ground Turkey		(GF) Cream of Chicken		(DF) Cheese
Quinoa		Rotisserie Chicken		Soup		Vegetable Choice
Pasta		Ham		Alfredo Sauce		Chow Mein Noodles
(GF) Pasta		Shrimp		Tomato Sauce		Fruit Choice
				Salsa		Nuts
						Herb Choice
						Black Olives

(GF) = Gluten Free (DF) = Dairy Free

Hawaiian Haystacks

Makes 4 Servings

INGREDIENTS

2 Cups White Rice, Cooked
3 Tablespoons Unsalted Butter
1/4 Cup White Onion, Diced 1/4 "
1 Garlic Clove, Minced
3 Tablespoons All Purpose Flour
2 Cups Chicken Stock
1/2 Cup Milk
1 1/2 Cup Cooked Rotisserie Chicken
   (shredded or diced)
1/2 Teaspoon Kosher Salt
1/4 Teaspoon Black Pepper

TOPPINGS

Celery, Diced
Carrot, Shredded
Pineapple, Fresh or Canned
Tomato, Diced
Green Onion, Finely Chopped
Avocado, Diced
Cheddar Cheese, Shredded
Chow Mein Noodles

DIRECTIONS

1 Cook rice to package directions.

2 In another medium sized saucepan on medium heat, melt the butter. Add the onion and garlic and sauté for 2-3 minutes, stirring with a whisk occasionally.

3 Add the flour and whisk continuously so the flour doesn't burn. Cook for 2 minutes to cook out the flour taste. Add the chicken stock and milk and bring to a simmer.

4 Add the chicken, salt and pepper and stir until creamy and well combined.

5 Prepare all of the toppings.

6 To plate, top your desired amount of rice with the chicken mixture and top with the toppings of your choice.

Taquitos Formula

1 BASE	+	1 PROTEIN	+	MIX INS
Flour Tortillas		Rotiserrie Chicken		Cheese Choice
ⒼⒻ Tortillas		Shredded Beef		ⒹⒻ Cheese
Corn Tortillas		Shredded Pork		Herb Choice
Wonton Skins		Shrimp		Gaucamole
Spring Roll Wrappers		Beans		Buffalo Hot Sauce
		Bacon		Salsa

ⒼⒻ = Gluten Free   ⒹⒻ = Dairy Free

Buffalo Chicken Taquitos

Makes 6 Taquitos

INGREDIENTS

6 Flour Tortillas
1 Cup Rotisserie Chicken, Shredded
1/2 Cup Mixed Italian Cheese or Four Cheese Blend
2 Ounces Cream Cheese
1/4 Cup Buffalo Hot Sauce
Ranch Dressing To Dip

FAN FAVORITE FORMULA

Base: Wonton Skins
Protein: Bacon
Mix Ins: Cheese, Gaucamole
& Bacon

DIRECTIONS

1 Preheat the oven to 400°F.

2 In a medium mixing bowl combine the rotisserie chicken, cheeses and hot sauce until all of the ingredients are well combined.

3 Place tortilla on a clean work surface and add 2 tablespoons of the chicken mixture to one edge of the tortilla.

4 Roll the edge of the tortilla tight over the filling and continue to roll to form a taquito.

5 You can place the taquito in a ziplock bag and freeze or cook at this point. Repeat steps 3-5 with all tortillas and chicken mixture.

6 To cook, place the taquitos seam side down on a foil lined baking sheet and bake for 10-15 minutes or until the filling is hot and the tortilla is slightly brown.

7 Serve with ranch dressing to dip.

Meatball *Formula*

1 BASE	+	**1 CRUMB**	+	**MAKE IT SAUCY**	+	**MIX INS**
Ground Beef		Bread Crumbs		Ketchup		Cheese Choice
Ground Turkey		(GF) Bread Crumbs		Worcestershire		(DF) Cheese
Ground Pork		Panko Crumbs		Sauce		Shredded Vegetables
Ground Lamb		(GF) Panko Crumbs		BBQ Sauce		Pickled Jalapeños
		Oatmeal		Pepper Jelly		Citrus Zest
				Pesto		Herb Choice
				Hoisin Sauce		

(GF) = Gluten Free (DF) = Dairy Free

GF Jalapeño Popper Meatballs

Makes 4 Servings

INGREDIENTS

1 Pound Ground Beef
1 Egg
1/4 Cup Shredded Cheddar Cheese
2 Tablespoons GF Panko Bread Crumbs
1 Teaspoon Worcestershire Sauce
1/2 Teaspoon Kosher Salt

1/4 Teaspoon Black Pepper
4 Ounces Cream Cheese, Cubed 1/2"
2 Tablespoons Tamed Jarred Pickled
   Jalapeño Peppers + More To Top
3 Tablespoons Vegetable Oil
3 Slices Bacon, Cooked, Crumbled

DIRECTIONS

1 Preheat oven to 400° F.

2 Place the ground beef into a mixing bowl and add the egg, cheddar cheese, panko, worcestershire sauce, salt and pepper.

3 Mix with your hands until just combined (be careful to not over mix).

4 Grab a golf ball sized amount of the meat mixture with clean hands and form the mixture into a ball. Using your thumb, imprint your finger in the middle of the ball to form an indent. Place one jalapeño and one cube of cream cheese into the well. Fold up the edges of the meat mixture to enclose the cream cheese and jalapeño. Repeat with all the remaining mixture.

5 Preheat a large cast iron skillet or ovenproof sauté pan over medium heat.

6 Add the vegetable oil and carefully place your meatballs in the pan (don't touch them for 5 minutes to sear). Flip over and sear for another 5 minutes. Remove from the stove and place the pan in the oven for 5 minutes.

7 Remove from the oven and top with crumbled bacon and pickled jalapeños.

Meatballs can easily be morphed into a meatloaf. Try it out and change it up!

+ Something
Creamy

+ Protein

+ Flavor
Blast

+ Spice
It Up

mix
+ in

+ Something
Sweet

Snack
Formulas

• • • • • • • • • • • • • • • • • •

PROTEIN BALLS

TOAST

SWEET DIP

SAVORY DIP

BAG IT UP

POPCORN

• • • • • • • • • • • • • • • • • •

WITH A TWIST

Lemon Protein Balls

Makes 2 Dozen

INGREDIENTS

1 Cup Cashews
1 Tablespoon Coconut Oil
1/2 Cup Honey
1 Teaspoon Lemon Zest

1 Tablespoon Lemon Juice
1 Teaspoon Vanilla Bean Paste or Extract
1 Tablespoon Chia Seeds
2 Cups Rolled Oats

DIRECTIONS

1. Place the cashews in a food processor or a blender with coconut oil. Blend until a paste starts to form. Transfer to a medium size mixing bowl.

2. Add the honey, zest and juice of the lemons, vanilla and chia seeds. Stir to combine. Add the oats and mix thoroughly.

3. Wet your fingers with water. Grab a golf ball sized amount of the oat mixture and roll in your hands to form a ball. Place in a large ziplock bag. Repeat with the remainder of the mixture until all of your protein balls are formed. Place the bag in the freezer.

4. You can eat these protein balls straight from the freezer or enjoy at room temperature.

Protein Balls Formula

1 BASE	+	1 CREAMY	+	SWEETENER	+	FLAVOR BLAST	+	MIX INS
Rolled Oats		Nut Butter		Honey		Spices		Chocolate Chips
GF Oats		Sun Butter		Agave Nectar		Citrus Zest		Shredded Coconut
Rice Cereal		Coconut Oil		Cocoa Powder		Extract		Chia Seeds
								Flax Seed
								Dried Fruit

GF = Gluten Free   DF = Dairy Free

Toast

Makes 1 Serving

Italian

INGREDIENTS

1 Bread, Sliced
1 Tablespoon Fig Jam
2 Pepperoni Slices
1 Tablespoon Cantaloupe, Diced
3 Mini Mozzarella Balls

PB and Chocolate

INGREDIENTS

1 Bread, Sliced
1 Tablespoon Peanut Butter
1/4 Banana, Sliced
1 Tablespoon Chocolate Chips

Chocolate Hazelnut

INGREDIENTS

1 Bread, Sliced
2 Tablespoons Chocolate Hazelnut
   Spread
2-3 Strawberries, Sliced

Savory Avocado

INGREDIENTS

1 Bread, Sliced
2 Tablespoons Avocado, Smashed
Savory Seasoning Blend

DIRECTIONS

1 Place your base on a clean work surface.

2 Spread the base evenly with spread.

3 Top with flavor blasts and toppings and serve.

This is one of my favorite go-to snack ideas. As long as you have the base you can create endless possibilities!

Toast Formula

1 BASE	+	1 SPREAD	+	FLAVOR BLAST	+	TOPPINGS
Sliced Bread		Butter		Cheese Choice		Herb Choice
ⓖⒻ Bread		Nut Butter		ⒹⒻ Cheese		Seasonings
ⒹⒻ Bread		Seed Butter		Meat Choice		Chocolate Chips
Rice Cakes		Avocado		Vegetable Choice		Shredded Coconut
Pita Bread		Jam		Fruit Choice		Honey
		Cream Cheese				
		Chocolate Hazelnut Spread				

ⓖⒻ = Gluten Free   ⒹⒻ = Dairy Free

Sweet Dip *Formula*

1 BASE	+	MIX INS	+	TOPPINIGS
Cool Whip		Extract		Shredded Coconut
Whip Cream		Cream Cheese		Fresh Fruit
(DF) Coco Whip		Dry Instant Pudding Mix		Canned Fruit
		Peanut Butter		Chocolate Chips
		Marshmallows		
		Fruit		

(GF) = Gluten Free   (DF) = Dairy Free

Pineapple Colada Dip

Makes 4 Servings

INGREDIENTS

1/2 Cup Crushed Pineapple, Drained
1 Cup Coco Whip
1/2 Teaspoon Vanilla Bean Paste or Vanilla Extract
2 Tablespoons Sweetened Coconut, Shredded, Toasted

SERVE WITH

Fruit, Graham Crackers or Cookies.

DIRECTIONS

1 In a small mixing bowl combine the pineapple, coco whip and vanilla.

2 Top with shredded coconut.

3 Serve with fruit or graham crackers.

If you haven't tried vanilla bean paste, you don't know what you are missing! Vanilla bean paste is like vanilla extract but it is thick and has actual vanilla beans infused into it. This is amazing for ALL baking recipes. Just use it the exact same as you would vanilla extract. It adds beautiful little vanilla beans all throughout your desserts, which makes it seem like you are cooking in a professional bakery!

Savory Dip *Formula*

1 BASE	+	MIX INS	+	FLAVOR BLAST
Canned Beans		Vegetable Choice		Hot Sauce
Cooked Lentils		Pico De Gallo		Herb Choice
		Bruschetta		Citrus Juice
		Pesto		Seasonings
				Cheese Choice
				ⒹⒻ Cheese
				Dressing Choice

ⒼⒻ = Gluten Free   ⒹⒻ = Dairy Free

Corn Relish Dip

Makes 10 Servings

INGREDIENTS

1 (15.5) Ounce Can Black Beans, Rinsed,
  Drained
1 Can Corn, Rinsed, Drained
1/2 Cup Prepared Pico De Gallo Salsa
1 Tablespoon Cilantro, Chopped
1 Lime, Juiced

FAN FAVORITE FORMULA

Base: Lentils
Mix Ins: Bruschetta
Toppings: Feta Cheese

(Serve with pita chips or
Tortilla Chips)

DIRECTIONS

1 Make sure your black beans and corn are drained and rinsed.

2 Add all of the ingredients to a medium size mixing bowl and mix to combine.

3 Serve with tortilla chips.

This is one of my favorite snacks or appetizer dishes. I even serve this dip in tortillas and make vegetarian tacos. You can top it on nachos, burrito bowls or even eggs.

Hummus In A Bag

Makes 4 Servings

HUMMUS INGREDIENTS

1 (15.5 ounce) Can Garbanzo Beans, Rinsed, Drained
1 Lemon, Juiced
1 Tablespoon Olive Oil
1/2 Teaspoon Kosher Salt
1/8 Teaspoon Black Pepper

TOPPINGS

Favorite Seasoning
Basil

HUMMUS DIRECTIONS

1 Toss all of the ingredients in a ziplock plastic baggie and remove the air.

2 Smash the beans with your hands until it becomes smooth.

3 Cut 1/4 " off the corner of the baggie with scissors and squeeze out the hummus in a serving dish or eat it straight out of the bag! Top with favorite seasoning and fresh basil.

PITA INGREDIENTS

1 Whole Wheat Pita
1 Teaspoon Olive Oil
Kosher Salt and Pepper (to taste)

PITA DIRECTIONS

1 Preheat oven to 450 F.

2 Cut pitas into 8 triangles. Tear the two layers apart to get 16 pita chips.

3 Drizzle with olive oil and season with salt and pepper.

4 Bake on a foil lined baking sheet for 7 minutes or until chips are toasted brown.

Bag it Up Formula

1 BASE	+	1 OIL	+	FLAVOR BLAST	+	TOPPINGS	+	ZIPLOCK BAG
Canned Beans		Avocado Oil		Citrus Zest		Seasonings		
		Olive Oil		Salt and Pepper		Herb Choice		
		Flavored Oils		Seasonings				
				Fresh Herbs				

GF = Gluten Free   DF = Dairy Free

GF Everything Seasoning Popcorn

Makes 6 Sevings

INGREDIENTS

2 Tablespoons Vegetable Oil
1/2 Cup Original Popcorn Kernels
2 Tablespoons Butter, Melted
1 Teaspoon Everything Seasoning or Savory Seasoning
1/4 Teaspoon Kosher Salt

DIRECTIONS

1 Preheat a medium size saucepan with a lid on medium heat.

2 Place the oil into pan and add popcorn kernels. Cover the pot with the lid.

3 Cook for about 3-5 minutes, shaking the pot occasionally until the popping subsides.

4 Pour the melted butter over the popped popcorn and then top with seasoning and kosher salt.

SAVORY FAN FAVORITE FORMULA

Base: Popcorn Kernels
Fat: Cocunut Oil
Flavor Blast Savory: Rosemary & Parmesan Cheese

SWEET FAN FAVORITE FORMULA

Base: Popcorn Kernels
Fat: Butter
Flavor Blast Sweet: Cinnamon & Butterscotch Chips

Popcorn is one of the easiest snacks and it is a total blank canvas. You can make it savory or sweet and it goes well with all flavors. You can make it on the stove or if you have a popcorn machine use that.

Popcorn *Formula*

1 BASE + **1 FAT** + **SAVORY FLAVOR BLAST** *or* **SWEET FLAVOR BLAST**

Popcorn Kernels

Olive Oil
Avocado Oil
Butter
Coconut Oil

Seasonings
Cheese Choice
(DF) Cheese
Herb Choice

Marshmallows
M&M's
Candy
Brown Sugar
Honey
Dried Fruit
Chocolate Chips
Spices

(GF) = Gluten Free   (DF) = Dairy Free

+ Something
Creamy

+ Flavor
Blast

+ Protein

+ Spice
It Up

mix
+ in

+ Something
Sweet

Dessert
Formulas

• • • • • • • • • • • • • • • •

COBBLER

CEREAL BALLS

CUPCAKES

ICE CREAM CAKE

COOKIE DOUGH

ICE CREAM SANDWICH

BROWNIES

TRIFLE

• • • • • • • • • • • • • • • •

Cobbler *Formula*

1 BASE	+	1 TOPPINGS	+	FLAVOR BLAST
Frozen Fruit		Cake Mix		Spices
Canned Fruit		(GF) Cake Mix		Nut Choice
Fresh Fruit		(DF) Cake Mix		Dried Fruit
		Cookie Mix		Caramel Sauce
				Chocolate Sauce
				Ice Cream
				(DF) Ice Cream

(GF) = Gluten Free   (DF) = Dairy Free

GF Easy Peach Cobbler

Makes 10 Servings

INGREDIENTS

Cooking Spray
2 (8) Ounce Jars Sliced Peaches, In Juice
1/2 Teaspoon Ground Cinnamon
     + 1/2 Teaspoon For Top
1 Box GF Yellow Cake Mix
1/3 Cup Milk
1/2 Cup Butter

TOPPINGS

Vanilla Ice Cream
Cinnamon

FAN FAVORITE FORMULA

Base: Canned Pineapple
Toppings: Yellow Cake Mix
Flavor Blast: Brown Sugar &
    Marachino Cherries

*Top the cake mix with the liquid and the butter and brown sugar and then cherries.

DIRECTIONS

1. Preheat the oven to 350°F. Spray a 9 x 12 baking dish with cooking spray.

2. Drain one of the jars of peaches. Place the drained peaches and the other jar of peach (with the juice) in the baking dish.

3. Spread the peaches out evenly. Top the peaches with the cake mix, ensuring all the peaches are covered and the cake mix is in one even layer.

4. Top with 1/2 teaspoon cinnamon and milk.

5. Cut the butter into very thin slices and place on top of the cake layer. Sprinkle with cinnamon.

6. Bake for 45 minutes. Top with ice cream and serve.

Did you ever think cake mix would make the best topping for a cobbler? Well it certainly does. Its one of my favorites!

Cereal Balls Formula

1 BASE	+	1 FAT	+	1 BINDER	+	MIX INS	+	FLAVOR BLAST
Cereal Choice		Butter		Marshmallows		Cake Mix		Sprinkles
(GF) Rice Cereal		(DF) Butter		(GF) Marshmallows		(GF) Cake Mix		Chocolate Chips
		Coconut Oil		Marshmallow		Coco Powder		Candy
				Cream		Instant Dry		Freeze Dried Fruit
				Nut Butters		Pudding Mix		Shredded Coconut
						Extract		

(GF) = Gluten Free   (DF) = Dairy Free

Cake Batter Cereal Balls

Makes 24 Balls

INGREDIENTS

1/2 Cup Coconut Oil or Butter
4 Cups Miniature Marshmallows
6 Cups Puffed Rice Cereal
1/2 Cup White Cake Mix
2 Tablespoons Multi Colored Sprinkles

DIRECTIONS

1   Melt the coconut oil or butter in a small saucepan over medium heat.

2   Add the marshmallows and stir continuously until they have melted. Add the cake batter and stir to combine.

3   Place the puffed rice cereal into a large mixing bowl. Add the marshmallow mixture to the rice cereal. Add the sprinkles and stir to combine. Let cool for 10 minutes.

4   Spray your hands with cooking spray to prevent sticking. Grab a golf ball size amount of the rice cereal mixture and roll to form a ball. Place in a re-sealable container.

5   Continue with the rest of the mixture.

Lemon Raspberry Cupcakes

Makes 2 Dozen

INGREDIENTS

1 Box White Cake Mix
1 Cup Instant Dry Lemon Pudding Mix
4 Egg Whites
1/3 Cup Vegetable Oil
1 1/4 Cup Water

DIRECTIONS

1 Preheat oven to 350 F. Place paper liners in muffin tin pan.

2 Combine cake mix and pudding mix in a mixing bowl fitted with a whisk attachment.

3 Add the eggs, oil and water and turn on low to mix for 1-2 minutes (scraping down the sides occasionally).

4 Place 1/4 cup of the batter into the muffin tins and bake for 15-20 minutes or until a toothpick comes out dry. Let cool completely.

5 Follow frosting directions. Frost each cupcake with frosting. Top with fresh raspberries.

FROSTING INGREDIENTS

8 Ounces Cream Cheese, Softened
1/2 Cup Butter, Softened
2 Pounds Powdered Sugar
1 Teaspoon Vanilla Bean Paste Or Vanilla Extract
1/4 Cup Fresh Raspberries

FROSTING DIRECTIONS

1 Add the cream cheese and butter to a mixing bowl fitted with a whisk attachment.

2 Cream the cream cheese and butter together for 1-2 minutes until combined.

3 With the mixer on low, slowly add the powdered sugar (a cup at a time).

4 Add vanilla bean paste and fresh raspberries and mix on low until combined.

Every time I make this recipe I have at least a handful of people ask me for it. It is great for cupcakes or to make in a cake so use it for both, you won't be disappointed.

Cupcakes *Formula*

I BASE	+	I FLAVOR BLAST	+	I LIQUID	+	FROST IT	+	TOPPINGS
Cake Mix		Dry Instant		Soda		Frosting		Fruit
(GF) Cake Mix		Pudding Mix:		Juice		Choice		Citrus Zest
(DF) Cake Mix		Vanilla		Water				Sprinkles
		Chocolate		Milk				Chocolate
		Lemon		(DF) Milk				Chips

(GF) = Gluten Free (DF) = Dairy Free

Ice Cream Cake *Formula*

1 BASE	+	ICE CREAM	FLAVOR BLAST	+	TOPPINGS
Cookies		Ice Cream Choice	Chocolate Syrup		Cookies
Brownie Crumbs		ⒹⒻ Ice Cream	Caramel Syrup		Candy Canes
Graham Crackers			Strawberry Syrup		Sprinkles
Macaroon Cookies			Marshmallow Cream		Candy
ⒼⒻ ⒹⒻ Cookies					Gummy Bears
					Cool Whip
					Whipped Cream

ⒼⒻ = Gluten Free   ⒹⒻ = Dairy Free

Mint Chocolate Ice Cream Cake

Makes 12 Servings

INGREDIENTS

1 Package Chocolate Sandwich Cookies, Crushed
1.5 Quarts Mint Chocolate Chip Ice Cream
1.5 Quarts Chocolate Ice Cream
1/4 Cup Chocolate Syrup
1/2 Cup Mint Candy

FAN FAVORITE FORMULA

Base: Macaroon Cookies
Flavor Blast: Rainbow Sherbert & Vanilla Bean Ice Cream
Toppings: Sprinkles & Cool Whip

DIRECTIONS

1 Place the oreos in a large ziplock bag and remove the air. With a rolling pin or skillet, smash the chocolate sandwich cookies to create crumbs.

2 Place half of the smashed cookies on the bottom of a springform pan.

3 Evenly scoop the chocolate ice cream on top of the cookies. Run a spoon under hot water. Using the spoon, spread the ice cream to create an even layer.

4 Top with half of the chocolate syrup and the remaining cookies.

5 Evenly scoop the mint chocolate chip ice cream on top of the cookies. Run a spoon under hot water. Using the spoon, spread ice cream to create an even layer. Top with chocolate syrup and mint candies.

6 Quickly place the cake into the freezer.

This is a family recipe that originated with coffee ice cream, chocolate ice cream, macaroon cookies, chocolate sauce and chocolate toffee bits on top. It is what we would have for our birthday and my whole family still loves it. We began morphing the recipe into versions for Thanksgiving, Christmas, Easter and even birthdays.

ⒼⒻ Chocolate Chip Cookies

Makes 2 Dozen

COOKIE DOUGH INGREDIENTS

1 Cup Butter Flavored Shortening or Butter
    (at room temperature)
1 Cup Brown Sugar, Packed
1/2 Cup Granulated Sugar
2 Eggs
1 Teaspoon Vanilla Bean Paste or Vanilla Extract
2 Cups ⒼⒻ Flour
1/4 Cup Dry Instant Vanilla Pudding Mix
1 Teaspoon Baking Soda
1 Teaspoon Baking Powder
1 Teaspoon Salt
1 1/2 Cup Semi Sweet Chocolate Chips

MIX INS

2 Tablespoons ⒼⒻ Candy
2 Tablespoons Potato Chips, Crushed
2 Tablespoons Toffee Bits

DIRECTIONS

1   Preheat the oven to 350° F.

2   In a mixing bowl cream together butter and sugars with a spatula (you can also do this is an electric mixer but you will get fluffier cookies if you do it by hand)

3   Stir in one egg at a time and mix to combine. Add vanilla and stir to combine.

4   Add flour, vanilla pudding mix, baking soda, baking powder, and salt and stir until combined.

5   Add chocolate chips and mix ins and stir to combine.

6   Grab about a golf ball sized amount of dough and place on a parchment lined baking sheet. You can fit 12 cookies on one sheet.

7   Bake for 11 minutes, remove from the oven and let cool.

Cookie Dough *Formula*

BASE	+	MIX INS	+	TOPPINGS
Chocolate Chip Cookie Dough (GF) Cookie Dough		Candy Chips Sandwich Cookies Cereal Shredded Coconut Nuts		Melted Chocolate Cinnamon Sugar Caramel Sauce Ice Cream (DF) Ice Cream

(GF) = Gluten Free (DF) = Dairy Free

Ice Cream Sandwich *Formula*

BASE	+	1 FLAVOR BLAST	+	DIP IT
Cookies:		Ice Cream:		Melted Chocolate
Chocolate Chip		Vanilla		White
Chocolate Chocolate		Chocolate		Dark
Chip		Strawberry		Milk
Peanut Butter		Rocky Road		Caramel Sauce
GF Snickerdoodle		Mint Chocolate Chip		
GF Cookie Choice		Cookies and Cream		

GF = Gluten Free   DF = Dairy Free

GF Snickerdoodle Ice Cream Sandwich

Makes 6 Sandwiches

COOKIE DOUGH INGREDIENTS

1 Cup Butter Shortening or Butter (at room temperature)
3/4 Cup Granulated Sugar
1 Egg, Whole
1/2 Teaspoon Vanilla Bean Paste or Vanilla Extract
1/4 Teaspoon Almond Extract
1 1/4 Cup GF Flour
1/2 Cup Dry Instant Vanilla Pudding Mix

1/4 Teaspoon Baking Soda
1/2 Teaspoon Baking Powder
1/2 Teaspoon Cream of Tarter
1/4 Teaspoon Salt
1 Teaspoon Cinnamon
Ice Cream, Rocky Road

COATING

1/2 Cup Sugar
1 Teaspoon Cinnamon

DIRECTIONS

1 Preheat the oven to 350 F.

2 In a mixing bowl cream together butter and sugar with a spatula (you can also do this is an electric mixer but you will get fluffier cookies if you do it by hand).

3 Stir in the egg and mix to combine. Add vanilla and almond extract and stir to combine.

4 Add flour, vanilla pudding mix, baking soda, cream of tarter, baking powder, salt and cinnamon and stir until combined.

5 Combine coating ingredients in a small bowl and set aside.

6 Grab about a golf ball sized amount of dough and place in the cinnamon sugar mixture and roll to coat.

7 Place cookie dough ball on a parchment lined baking sheet (you can fit 9 cookies on one sheet).

8 Bake for 11 minutes, remove from oven and let cool.

9 Place a scoop of the rocky road ice cream on one cookie and top with another cookie to form a sandwich.

Gooey Brownies

Makes 24 Servings

INGREDIENTS

Cooking Spray
2 Boxes Brownie Mix
2 Eggs
2/3 Cup Water
2/3 Cup Oil
1 Cup Chocolate Chips

TOPPINGS

Vanilla Ice Cream

HOLIDAY FAN FAVORITE FORMULA

Base: (GF) Brownie Mix
Mix Ins: Chocolate Chips & Peppermint Extract
Toppings: Peppermint Ice Cream

DIRECTIONS

1 Preheat the oven to 325 F.

2 Add brownie mix, egg, water, oil and chocolate chips to a medium sized mixing bowl and mix to combine.

3 Spray a 9x10 baking dish with cooking spray and fill the pan with brownie mixture.

4 Bake for 40-45 minutes. Top with ice cream while still warm. Serve immediately.

Brownies are one of my favorite treats! Find a brand you really enjoy and top it with your favorite toppings! A trick with brownies is to cut them with a plastic knife. The brownies will cut perfectly and not stick to the knife.

Brownies *Formula*

I BASE	+	MIX INS	+	TOPPINGS
Brownie Mix		Chocolate Chips		Cookies
(GF) Brownie Mix		Caramel Chips		Candy
		Butterscotch Chips		Frosting
		Extract		Caramel
		Peanut Butter		Chocolate Sauce
		Dry Instant Pudding Mix		Ice Cream

(GF) = Gluten Free (DF) = Dairy Free

Trifle Formula

1 BASE	+	SOMETHING CREAMY	+	FLAVOR BLAST
Cake		Pudding Choice		Candies
(GF) Cake		Whipped Cream		Chocolate Sauce
Brownies		Whip Topping		Caramel Sauce
Cookies		(DF) Coco Whip		Berry Sauce
		Ice Cream		Peanut Butter

(GF) = Gluten Free   (DF) = Dairy Free

Pumpkin Caramel Trifle

Makes 10 Servings

INGREDIENTS

1 Box Spice Cake Mix (follow package directions and ingredients)
1/2 Cup Instant Dry Vanilla Pudding Mix
2 Cups Milk
1 Container Coco Whip
Caramel Sauce (to drizzle)
1/2 Cup Canned Pumpkin Puree
1 Cup Chocolate Toffee Bits

FAN FAVORITE FORMULA

Base: Brownies
Something Creamy: Chocolate Pudding, Whipped Cream
Flavor Blast: Toffee bits, Chocolate Sauce & Caramel Sauce

DIRECTIONS

1. Make the spice cake according to the package directions. Cook in two 9 inch cake pans and let cool completely.

2. In a medium mixing bowl combine pudding mix with milk and whisk together for 3 minutes until pudding becomes thick. Stir in the pumpkin puree. Set in the fridge for 10 minutes.

3. Crumble one of the cakes in the bottom of a trifle dish.

4. Layer all of the pudding mixture on top of the crumbled cake.

5. Drizzle with caramel sauce and half of the toffee bits.

6. Crumble the other cake on top of the caramel and toffee bits.

7. Top with the coco whip and spread evenly, covering the whole surface. Finish with a drizzle of caramel and remaining toffee bits.

Trifle is a great holiday dessert.
To watch this recipe live head over to our YouTube Channel, Allergy Reality.

Formula Favorites

Formula Notes

Formula Notes

A Special Thanks

From Meg:

I want to thank my sweet husband who inspires me everyday and encourages me to do what I love. You are my rock and my backbone for all that I do. To my kiddos, Logan and Hudson, for keeping me going and giving me the best gift in life: to be their momma. You both bring me so much joy and happiness. I want to also thank my own momma for always being there for me and encouraging me to write my own cookbook. Your sacrifice and unconditional love has been an inspiration throughout my life.

A big thanks to Coral; I couldn't have done any of this without her, and for riding on this crazy journey with me. For all my family and friends thank you for all your support.

From Coral:

I have so much to be grateful for. The influence and positivity from those around me has made me the positive person that I am today. My mother has taught me from such a young age never to play the victim. This principle has carried me through many difficult times, and has made me a better person. This cookbook is a testament of this very principle. Thank you, mom, for all the love and support.

A huge thank you to my husband who believes in me and encourages me to never give up. For my four children Gavin, Aliyah, Chanelle, and Sadie, who are so excited for all that I do and understand that making a positive difference in the world is so important and takes a lot of time. A special thank you to my sister, Raela, who is my right hand (perhaps because I am left handed). She is a perfect example of service and being there for anyone in need. I can not forget my sister-in-law, Sheri, who I call and run to for every crazy idea and design.

A HUGE thank you to Megan for being my sidekick in all of our wild and exciting adventures. You have helped me to realize that I can do anything, and together we are unstoppable.

From Both of Us:

And of course thank YOU for supporting us and buying our first cookbook...
Stay tuned, there is way more to come...

+ **Something Creamy**

+ **Protein**

+ **Flavor Blast**

+ **mix in**

+ **Spice It Up**

+ **Something Sweet**

10/18

Made in the USA
Middletown, DE
15 August 2018